PRAISE FOR ROGER ROSENBLATT AND
Anything Can Happen

—〰—

"Rosenblatt sets himself apart from his rivals by not being too clever for his own good. He's real. His advice rocks."
                                    —*The Toronto Star*

"[Rosenblatt's] wisdom and wit make for advice that is more applicable and more hilarious than Morrie's. Really."
                                    —*Detroit Free Press*

"With his clipped, clever drollery, his royal wryness, Roger Rosenblatt accentuates all of life's dark imponderables with a wonderful tint of humorous resignation."
                                    —*Fort Worth Star-Telegram*

"Rosenblatt is bright, funny and tells it like it is."
                                    —*St. Louis Post-Dispatch*

"The best thing about reading an essay by Rosenblatt is that he makes you think. Some writers leave you laughing. He leaves you trying to make sense of the nonsensical. Not always easy, but always intriguing."

—*Town & Country*

"[Rosenblatt] goes for laughs, but there's always a grain of truth there." —*The Times-Picayune* (New Orleans)

"Many of the 60-odd short pieces . . . sparkle and sting with Rosenblatt's trademark droll wit." —*Tulsa World*

"Roger Rosenblatt is one of our most gifted essayists—wise, funny, and insightful." —Tom Brokaw

"Some of the most profound and stylish writing in America today." —William Safire

"A national treasure." —*United Press International*

Anything Can Happen

ALSO BY ROGER ROSENBLATT

Rules for Aging

Where We Stand

Black Fiction

Children of War

Witness

Life Itself

Coming Apart

The Man in the Water

Consuming Desires

Anything Can Happen

Notes on My Inadequate Life
and Yours

ROGER ROSENBLATT

A HARVEST BOOK • HARCOURT, INC.
Orlando   Austin   New York   San Diego   Toronto   London

Requests for permission to make copies of any part of
the work should be mailed to the following address:
Permissions Department, Harcourt, Inc.,
6277 Sea Harbor Drive, Orlando, Florida 32887-6777.

www.HarcourtBooks.com

Library of Congress Cataloging-in-Publication Data
Rosenblatt, Roger.
Anything can happen: notes on my inadequate life and yours/
Roger Rosenblatt.—1st ed.
p.   cm.
ISBN 0-15-100866-3
ISBN 0-15-602955-3 (pbk.)
1. American wit and humor. I. Title.
PN6165.R67 2003
818'.5402—dc21   2002153234

Text set in Bembo
Display set in Schneidler
Designed by Cathy Riggs

Printed in the United States of America

First Harvest edition 2004
A C E G I K J H F D B

for Carl, Amy, John, Wendy, and Harris
exceptionally adequate children

CONTENTS

The girls were so frightened. You know how children are? "Suppose we're taken into the air?" And Doctor Paynter laughed and laughed. "That can't happen." And on the way home, I thought about Dan dying. We walked through the red rain. And I thought about you killing. And we stepped into great red puddles. And I said to the girls, "I will now give you a great lesson." Because the girls must be taught. "Anything can happen." That is the most horrid fact about living. Anything can happen. And we were home. And I looked at the house. And I looked at the red ocean. And it had all happened here. What we had been. What we had become. What we were. —LYDIE BREEZE by John Guare

Don't blame me. I didn't make the world. I barely live in it.
—Oscar Levant to John Garfield in HUMORESQUE

Take Two

I'd like to do that again, if I could, Mr. DeMille.

We haven't got all day.

I know, I'm sorry. But I think I could make it work so much better this time. One more take?

The first was fine. Time is money.

Yes, yes. Time is money. But there is so much more I could bring to the lines with a second try. I've been thinking about the part a lot. Me as a child, for instance. I was much happier than I played it. You know? And the cruelty of my folks? Their blunders? Their neglect? That wasn't exactly right, either. They were just people, you know? I probably haven't done much better as a parent.

Or worse.

Or worse! Exactly! That's what I mean, Mr. DeMille. If I could just do it over, I would make a few corrections. The marriage scenes, the scenes at work. And I wouldn't thrash around as if I regretted every move I'd ever made, either. You know? That's just acting. I didn't come close to regretting much in my life. I really liked my life. I was just wallowing in a mood.

Like the rest of us.

You said it, Mr. DeMille. Like the rest of us. And as for the lonely times—the times I dwelt on?—well, they were also the most useful. You know? Like those Sunday afternoons in winter when I wandered the city like a ghost. I played those scenes as if I'd been abandoned forever when the truth was that the time by myself made me self-confident, kind of brave. So, you see, if I could...

Do you realize what you're talking about? You're talking about reshooting the whole picture! You must be nuts!

I just don't want to leave the wrong impression.

Everybody leaves the wrong impression, kiddo. Don't worry your pretty little head about it. Oh, wow. The story was better than you played it. Happier, kinder, sweeter. Big deal.

That's it, Mr. DeMille. That's what I mean.

And if we rolled again, you'd play it happier, kinder, sweeter.

I would! I would!

And get it right this time.

Absolutely!

Know what your trouble is, kid?

What, Mr. DeMille? What's my trouble?

You don't know bupkis about movies.

My Bear

My bear is of the polar variety. He squats at the other end of my kitchen table every morning, and he stares at me with his black, black eyes. He does not move, but I hear his even snorting. *Gnnn, gnnn, gnnn.* Like that, in a low guttural snort that is neither threatening nor amiable. If my kitchen window is open, the breeze will flutter the tips of his white fur. He is seven or eight feet tall (I haven't measured). There is nothing immediately alarming about him; yet, once I sit down, I am afraid to move.

He has something to do with my innermost fears—anyone can see that. Or with my mood swings. Once I suggested to him that he might be a bipolar bear, but he showed no amusement. I offered him Frosted Flakes one morning, too. I do not think that bears have a sense of humor.

I cannot recall when he first appeared—some years ago, certainly. It was not in the morning that I first saw him but rather one midnight, when, for lack of sleep, I came downstairs for a snack of Jell-O and there he was, glowing white in the light of a full moon. I sat and stared at him as he stared at me. Eventually, I got sleepy and retired.

Lately, he has stirred from the kitchen, where he spends his days, and has moved up to the bedroom at night, where he squats at the foot of my bed. He seems to wish to be with me night and day. I do not know what it is about me that attracts him. If he wanted to kill me, he could have done that long ago. Bears may look cute, but they are ferocious. One swipe of the paw and I would be scattered around the room like so many pieces of paper.

One night I decided to flatter him, but it made no impression. One night I presented a philosophical monologue to him—something that yoked the fates of bears and men together in harmony. He did not so much as blink. One night I cursed him out. I don't know where I got the courage, but I even raised my hand to him. I hardly need tell you that there was no reaction.

Here's my problem: If he establishes his influence in my household, as he has pretty much done already, how long will it be before he follows me outside?

How long before he accompanies me to the newsstand or the grocer's? Think of the awkwardness, the embarrassment. He is not Harvey, after all; he's not invisible. And he is certainly not sweet-natured or wise. Soon, no one will come near me out of fright.

I am thinking of calling the ASPCA. Perhaps tomorrow, or the day after that. My bear is an unwanted animal, is he not? It is the business of the ASPCA, their duty, to take unwanted animals and treat them humanely. I would not want him hurt. Yes, I will definitely call the ASPCA by the end of the week, or early next at the latest, and tell them to please rid me of my bear, my beautiful big white polar bear.

Lecture to One Suffering Yet Another Identity Crisis

—ᴡᴡ—

You strive to know yourself, and you are convinced that such knowledge derives from certain anticipations, from knowing how you will react if she does this, if he does that, or if this reward comes your way, or that calamity. You believe that self-knowledge comes from practice: You know how you will behave if you are rejected or if you have a surfeit of success because it has all happened before. You repeat yourself. That's who you are.

Or, if you know your limitations, you will say: "I know how much I can drink or how far I will go." And you'll call that knowing yourself—as if you were a car with so much gasoline inside you or a bottle with a definite capacity.

Or you'll focus on your taste or appetites. "That simply isn't me," you'll say, while trying on a hat. "Not me. I'm a different sort of hat." And that's true.

You are a different hat, of a certain size and material, to be worn in one kind of weather and not another.

Or you believe that you are several selves—a torch singer, a bruiser, a lewd woman, a mouse of a man. You're not everybody, of course. No one is everybody. But you're several people. You know that. So you love your several selves. That's who you are. Or you hate your several selves and see yourself as the enemy. That's who you are.

There *is* another way of looking at this question of identity. Find a point outside yourself—less idiosyncratic, less self-referential, more connected to people you have never met. It isn't hard, really.

In a hotel recently, I saw a cardboard sign posted on an easel in the lobby announcing a meeting that day of a group involved with the economics of veterinary medicine. The event was titled "Practice and Progress." In the upper right-hand corner of the sign was a yellow Post-it note that read PUT THIS UP IMMEDIATELY!

And I pictured the person to whom that Post-it was directed—he or she who waited for orders from hotel management to put up cardboard signs for hotel meetings. And having received the orders, that person acted on them promptly, lest he or she lose the job and paycheck to someone who followed orders faster and better. So this person, whoever he or she was, would, upon receipt of the daily orders, position the poster on the easel in the center of the hotel lobby where all could see it, especially those involved with the organization on the economics of veterinary medicine.

And he or she, consciously or unconsciously, would also leave the yellow Post-it in the upper right-hand corner as a sign, however small, that he or she existed at all.

Once I had pictured this person, I knew who I was.

On Aristocracy

In 1993, on assignment for *Vanity Fair*, I went to Sudan with Sabastião Salgado, the great photographer of human suffering, to write about the "lost boys"— those who had fled their villages in the north to escape the Khartoum government soldiers. Over 100,000 of these boys had made a biblical trek through the relentless heat, the semi-desert cold, the swollen rivers. They had eluded the animals that hunted them, and they had survived disease and famine. Salgado and I came to a spot near Nattinga where about four hundred boys were beginning to set up camp. They were searching for water and building their *tukuls,* or huts, when we arrived—two white men who might have dropped in from Mars. But when they saw us, they stopped whatever else they were doing and made two beds for us out of *kam,* a very hard wood that the Nuer use for spears. They made us beds, and they made us a table, and they made sure that we, their guests, were taken care of. At night they played music on a handmade lyre, a *rabala,* and they gathered round us to tell folktales, by flashlight, in the cold darkness.

When anyone asks me if I have ever met a true aristocrat, I tell them this story.

What Bothers Me

—*m*—

1. Why, in "This Little Piggy Went to Market," which is a mere five lines long, do two lines end in "home."

2. Why do priests, ministers, and rabbis only get together in jokes?

3. Where exactly is Magnesia?

4. Are members of the Hammond family organ donors?

5. Who was Absorbine Sr.?

6. Is there an illegal pad? Tell me there's an illegal pad.

7. E I E I O?

Advice to Those About to Acquire a Rembrandt

———

Always look at it as it might appear in its average moments—not as it might glow in the light-dance of the fireplace or burn from within on a fall Sunday morning when the amalgamation of the sun's rays blasts red upon those fat Dutch cheeks or as you would make it glow when you return home flushed with one victory or another, or with wine. None of that.

Rather think: What will this Rembrandt look like at 2:45 on a February afternoon when you have run out of toilet paper and the roof leaks and a horse has just kicked in your kitchen door for the fun of it. And when there's a dead squirrel stuck high in the chimney. Consider moments such as these, when you are about to acquire your Rembrandt.

And yes. She *is* as lovely as a Rembrandt.

Tyranny for Beginners

Lyndon Johnson badgered Hubert Humphrey into killing a deer on a visit to Johnson's Texas ranch, then he sent the vice president the severed head of the animal as a reminder of his power over him.

That's really all there is to it. The first thing a tyrant learns is to make people do what they do not want to do—not by using physical force but rather by cajoling or teasing or manipulating the intellect, so that they not only lose all self-respect but also become so weakened in spirit that they believe the tyrant alone can lead them on the right path.

The time you made someone else apologize for something that you did wrong, for instance. That was a start.

Don't Take Your Soul
to New England

———

Your mind, yes. You can take your mind to New England without doing it any great damage. But your soul—up there in the dark pines and the frozen water and the lengthening shadows of small mountains over empty fields and suicidal cows, it's no place for a soul. Read Hawthorne, the Mathers, and the Lowells, if you don't believe me. Spars, spires, white clapboard Congregational churches screaming murder in the night. And Harvard Square at twilight, when the zombies hang around the bookstores before they head for your porch. Do not speak of it. Makes one's blood freeze.

Stopping by Words
on a Snowy Evening

—⁓—

Can it be possible? We've lost ourselves again? When we had such a nice brand-new compass and this GPS? Well, *c'est la vie*. What I meant to say, the thing I meant to say was, "Look—our snow." But all I said was something about having miles to go before I sleep.

On Your Conduct
at the Dinner Party

—ᴍ—

Nothing you said struck a bell. You named a name, but no one knew it. You cited a date. No one had heard of the occasion. Nobody was familiar with the town you mentioned—or with the country that the town was in, for that matter. And while you were admirably forceful in stating your positions on the issues, not a single one of them provoked the slightest reaction. At last, you changed the subject. But that engendered no response, either. One by one, heads turned away from you in boredom, disgust, or bafflement, leaving you to yourself at the table.

Well done.

My Stump Speech

—m—

Gesundheit. *[Applause]* My favorite flavor is vanilla chocolate chip. And I'm from the South. *[Applause]* I'm from the great state of New Hampshire. *[Applause]* Madonna will be with us in a moment. But first, you are going to win the lottery. What do you think of that? Subway heroes are both sandwiches and vigilantes. What do you think of that? *[Applause]* I got drunk last night, but I'm sorry. I blame it on the evil Dewar's. *[Laughter]* Does anybody read Edmund Spenser anymore? *[Sighs and a smattering of applause]* Pupu platter *[Laughter]* Death to the farmers! You know, when I was a boy, Ben Franklin was dead. What do you think about that? I really want to know. I feel your pain. I hear your anger. I smell your dirty underwear. *[Laughter, cries of Oh!]* Whoopie Goldberg will be with us in a minute. It's usually about here that I pause and look up to see if anybody is listening to a word I'm saying. But I know better. Shall we go on?

[Cries of You bet!*]* When I was a boy, I loved going huntin' with my three beautiful children: Kelly, Kelleye, and Genipher. We'd go out and shoot and shoot until every dog and cat in the neighborhood lay paws-up on the sidewalk. Which reminds me: Let's bomb China. If elected, I promise to bomb the shit out of China. *[Applause]* She's my daughter. *[Slap]* She's my father. *[Slap]* She's my daughter *and* my father. *[Slap]* Let's all sing: "We'll kiss again/Like this again." Less employment, more enjoyment! Bomb China! *[Applause, cheers]* Yet I come as a man of La Manchuria. I walk softly but I carry a big stump. Yes, I had sex with sects. So what? Wouldn't you? *[Laughter]* But taxes are too low. As my great aunt, the king of France, used to say: "It's the taxonomy, stupide! Where's the boeuf? Je would like to know." Let's bomb France! Let's bomb Social Security and our children and grandchildren. *[Cheers, hoots of joy]* And everyone is goin' to have a good-payin' job. And there'll be twenty women in my cabinet, and twenty more in my cupboard, and they'll all be cute as buttons. Hey! Uncle Ben! That's right, you. *[Applause starts to mount]* Uncle Ben up there in the balcony. Uncle Ben of Uncle Ben's Converted Rice House, will you please sit down? *[Earnest applause]* Finally, let me say: Val Kilmer. Hello? *[Ovation]*

On Class Distinctions

You can tell a burgher from a peasant by the way his belly quivers.

You can tell a professor from a burgher by the watery leer in his eyes.

You can tell an aristocrat from a professor by the relatively few times he refers to his work.

But the street they walk on looks like all streets—the same sidewalks, trees, sewers, the same rubbish.

Shorter Than Bacon's

On Politeness

Politeness is gentility in everything that does not matter. No one ever said: "Please excuse me if I ruin your life."

On Conservatives

Conservatives conserve what liberals have won for them. You'd think they'd be more grateful.

On Rich Men

A rich man is always accorded more honor than a talented one because people understand money.

On Love

Shortly after one falls in love, one wants to be naked with the person one loves. Naked. Meaning exposed, vulnerable, unprotected. That should tell you something about love.

On Despair

Do not force your despair upon others. It isn't that they will not sympathize or wish you rid of it. But it is a lot to ask of people to add your despair to their own. People are not that strong.

On Heroes

You have to risk your life to be one. But there are lots of ways to do that. One can be a hero who seeks nothing he has gladly left behind. You, for instance. When you walked away from *them*. You were a hero.

On Journalists

Journalists are alarmists by nature. *That's* why they're untrustworthy.

On Cleverness

A French writer—Sartre, I think—was asked the age-old question about what he would take from his house if the place were on fire. He said he'd take the fire. Not his wife, not his children, not his pets, books, letters, or insurance policy. The fire. That is a good example of being too clever by half.

On Women and Men

One never hears a woman say: "I wasted my life." From which one may conclude that *(a)* women do not waste their lives; *(b)* they are too considerate to say so; *(c)* men are ridiculous.

On Censorship

I have no way of knowing this, of course, but I would bet that every civilization that destroyed itself began to do so when someone in power demanded to know what the people were reading.

On Assisted Living

I could use some.

A Song for Jessica

—⁓—

If you're happy and you know it, clap your hands, because you're way ahead of the game, and there's something to be said for the perseverance of the itsy-bitsy spider and the weasel who went pop. Of course, from time to time the bough is liable to break, Humpty-Dumpty will fall, London Bridge will fall, all will fall down. But the wheels on the bus do go round round round, and when you row row row your boat merrily merrily merrily merrily, life *is* but a dream.

New Year's at Luchow's

Luchow's was a famous old German restaurant in downtown New York, situated just about where Irving Place and Fourteenth Street make a T. It was a bustling spot all year long, but especially at Christmastime when the proprietors propped up a huge Christmas tree for all to admire, and a hefty group called the Oom Pah Band tooted "O Tannenbaum" as the customers sang along. Diamond Jim Brady proposed to Lillian Russell in Luchow's, offering her a suitcase filled with one million dollars if she'd consent. (She didn't.) That's the sort of place Luchow's was until it closed some years ago.

My parents used to take my brother, Peter, and me to Luchow's every so often, even though my father suspected the restaurant of having been a Nazi hangout during the war. There we went, nonetheless, to stuff our faces and gape at celebrities. I saw Jackie Gleason there once, looking like the comics' Little

King, and leading a retinue including Jack Lescoulie, of mellow memory, among the crowded tables. That was not on New Year's Day. My family never went anywhere on New Year's Day, though for two years running Peter and I, while never going anywhere, still managed to spend the day at Luchow's.

You see, when my brother was in high school, he acquired his own telephone, the number of which was but one digit removed from Luchow's. At first he was annoyed by this coincidence, as calls for Luchow's and calls for my brother came in at a ratio of twenty to one. So, eventually tiring of the phrase "Wrong number," he began to accept a few reservations. This was a cruel prank, to be sure, but partly justified in his, and later in my own mind, for our being on the receiving rather than the phoning end of the calls.

Returning from graduate school one Christmas vacation, I was delighted to discover my brother's new enterprise and immediately joined his restaurant business with all the high spirits of the season. Embellishing his practice of taking reservations straight, I would ask—whenever someone called requesting a table for eight, for example—if the caller also wanted chairs. In no instance, and there were dozens, did the people calling for reservations treat my question as odd. As long as they thought they had Luchow's on the phone, everything was jake.

During spring vacation we adorned our business further by adding a touch of professionalism. Because of frequent requests for the Luchow's headwaiter, we learned that the man's name was Julius, which Peter, for reasons of his own, insisted on converting to Hoolio and adopting it whenever a call came in. I would answer the phone and transfer the call to Hoolio, who would do most of the talking in a Spanish-German accent so difficult to penetrate that requests for tables—and chairs—often took ten minutes.

We then began to push things a bit, in part to test the limits of human credulity. We asked people if they wished to be seated in the Himmler Room or if they wanted to try our special "Luftwaffles" instead of rolls. ("They're light as a Messerschmitt," we would boast.) We asked them if they would care to try Luchow's "blitzes." These, we explained, were blintzes dropped onto one's plate from a great height. There were long pauses at the other end of the line when we would ask such things, but the answers, when they arrived, were always polite and sincere. Once we asked a fellow if he'd mind taking a table for three instead of four—one of his party could eat elsewhere, and they could all regroup for coffee. He declined our suggestion, but he had considered it.

Our best customers were big shots who presumed a favored relationship with the restaurant. These customers made their reservations in barks: "Julius. Mr. Van Kamp. For two. Tonight. Good." Whenever Hoolio would hear such talk, he would warm up the tone immediately, keeping Van Kamp on the line for interminable periods as he, Hoolio, confessed his deepest, most intimate problems to his personal customer. After a while, Hoolio would get around to the fact that he was broke. Perhaps Mr. Van Kamp could see fit to make Hoolio a gift of five hundred dollars as a token of their long friendship. No? In that case there was no table for Van Kamp.

As these transactions continued over the summer, my brother and I became a little ashamed of the havoc we thought we were causing. We did not stop altogether, however, until the following Christmas vacation when we started asking people if they would mind being seated on the roof, where we had set up a cold buffet. This was late December, and the temperature in New York often fell below zero when it wasn't snowing. Still, there were one or two takers for our rooftop seats—though that was not the event that persuaded us to give up the restaurant business.

That event occurred on New Year's Day itself when a sugar-voiced lady phoned in the morning to cancel a reservation for lunch. Hoolio was furious. How were we supposed to run a restaurant—he told her—if everyone called up to cancel reservations? No, madam, it was impossible. Under no circumstances could we accept her cancellation. When the woman apologized and started to change her mind, we felt it was time to close up shop.

Yo, Weatherman

—w—

I have trouble understanding your terms. When you are exceedingly cold to me but do not really mean it, is that the wind-chill factor? And when you appear to love me more than you do, I assume that's the heat and humidity index. Or is this all bullshit, you cheerful son-of-a-bitch, and you don't give a rat's ass how I feel?

The Men's Room Wall: A Fantasy

—m—

GOOD LUCK, EVERYBODY!

I LOVE MY BOSS.

LONG LIFE TO AFRICAN AMERICANS,
ASIANS, AND LATINOS!

IF YOU WANT A GOOD TIME,
CALL A THEATER OR A MUSEUM.

HURRAY FOR PENISES AND VAGINAS!

THE SWASTIKA IS A VILE SYMBOL.

GO IMPROVE YOURSELF.

SICK—MY DUCK.

Beautiful Houses

—⁓—

Beautiful houses give me the creeps; though, of course, I never say that to the owners. I say: What a beautiful house! This is beautiful, and that is beautiful. This half bath is beautiful. And that dining alcove is beautiful. And I do not wish to omit mention of the latticework on the gazebo, the wainscoting in the attic, the built-ins, the one closet (it's a room in itself) for him, and the one for her...while in my foul, lying heart I seek the bottom of the armoire (what a beauty!) in which to hide or die.

This is not fair- or broad-minded of me, I know. There's nothing morally or ethically wrong with a beautiful house. It's not a sin to have four working fireplaces or a kitchen to die for. To have called upon Messrs. Williams and Sonoma in order to display a wooden encasement for a set of knives (twelve) or a chrome toaster (three slices) does not a criminal make. I do know that. And perhaps I would feel differently if

I myself lived in a beautiful house with a step-down living room and a medium-size media room, rather than the house I do live in, where the pictures pop off the walls spontaneously because the walls are made of thickened paint.

I leveled the kitchen floor (whoever put these tiles in originally did it all wrong, mister). I had the chimney rebuilt (the house leans, the chimney leans, mister). The paint on the doors is cracked in so many directions, it looks like a Pollock. The lawn, what there is of it, resembles the skin of a shaved horse. And the porch is sinking. And the gutters are feeding water back toward the foundation. And the floorboards don't line up because there have been a dozen room shifts since the house went up in 1882.

And now—because the house has been revealed as old—you expect me to say that I find all its deteriorations beautiful, more beautiful than any house where the window frames are not rhomboids and the doors close flush. But I do not. It drives me wild and wastes my time to be forever shoring up the place or panicking like some desperate villager in Mexico when the floods have risen to the second story. Frankly, I half expect the arrival of a flood, the spill-off from a hurricane. The house is near the sea.

And if a flood should happen, something like the hurricane of 1938, my old house will undoubtedly be whacked into the bay, and so will all the beautiful houses around here. Then everyone will have to rebuild. The people who occupy the beautiful houses will make new houses that are even more beautiful. And I will make a beautiful house, too—just as beautiful as theirs—and it will give me the creeps. But what can I do? It is impossible to reconstruct a house such as the one I've got now. It simply could not be done, which is, of course, my point.

Lines Written Nowhere Near Tintern Abbey

—⁓—

On How to Tell You've Been at a Dinner Party
with Witty People
    For no reason at all, you feel like hosing down a
butcher shop.

On Why People Get Married
    Form rescues content. That's why.

On Madness: A Primer
    First, ask about her former lovers.

On Laughter
    A great big laugh ends in a sigh. I don't understand
that, but I thought I'd mention it.

On Learning to Hate English Literature
    The pathetic fallacy is not a fallacy; metaphysical

poetry is not metaphysical; Henry James is hardly worth the time; and a whale road is not a kenning. It's a whale road.

On Ambition

"The real is a wilderness/that ambition calls a garden," wrote Harold Brodkey. It could be true, even useful, but only if you prefer a garden to a wilderness.

On Zealotry

The zealot who stands on his head sees everything that the man who stands upright sees. So it's never a good idea to argue with him in terms of the world he takes in. You just have to note that he's standing on his head.

On the Nature of Scholarship

A scholar of renown wrote a love letter to a lady he wished to marry. It consisted of much rational thought and many references to theology. Certain spaces were deliberately left blank in the text. He then handed the letter to his secretary for typing with the instructions, as regarding the blank spaces, "insert endearments here." This is a true story.

On Plagiarists and Their Apologists
Between the bubonic and the plague, how to choose?

On Institutions
Institutions do not care for particulars. That is why you must stay as far away from them as possible, my sweet particular.

On God
Montesquieu said: "If triangles had a god, it would have three sides." My kind of God.

To One Who Asks Why I Am in Such a Rage
The usual, friend. Injustice.

To Hannibal Lecter
What's eating *you?*

Twenty Things One Would
Like to See in Movies

—◦◦◦—

1. The Amish family is extremely nasty and abusive.

2. The African-American cop is not the first one killed.

3. No dances, no wolves.

4. The central male figure is not an architect.

5. No one says: "Get your butt in here (or out of here)."

6. The serial killer leaves no clues, does not get in touch with the pursuing detective, and does not want to be caught.

7. We enter a black inner-city neighborhood and no boom box is playing rap.

8. A woman lawyer is abysmally stupid and incompetent.

9. A man travels through several dimensions and is ignored in every one of them.

10. A green beret commando is ordered not to go back across enemy lines to rescue his buddies. He obeys.

11. "Only a *flesh* wound? This is killing me!"

12. A major rock star plays an aspiring rock star and in his or her first performance flops big time and is booed off the stage.

13. No one says: "Big time."

14. A man digs deep into a crime of the past and comes up with nothing.

15. A reporter is polite, sensitive, smart, and honest—and does not get the story.

16. A hotel cleaning lady opens the hotel room

door, discovers a murder victim, and calmly calls the police.

17. A crusty old classics teacher is feared and mocked by the students in a prep school where he has taught for forty years, and he turns out to be a pederast, a plagiarist, and an embezzler.

18. A policeman is not known and hated for doing things "his way." He does things everybody else's way.

19. There's a scene about a Bingo game, in which the winners cry out: "I won!" Nobody in the film, especially those using computers, ever says: "Bingo!"

20. The police trace a phone call from a criminal in a split second—no waiting. As soon as they pick up the phone, they yell: "We've got him!"

Odes for a Rainy Afternoon

—*m*—

On Jumping to Conclusions
People use the phrase "jumping to conclusions" as an expression of disapproval—as if to jump to a conclusion is a silly and fruitless thing to do. Yet, when one spies a conclusion, what else is there to do but jump to it?

To a Friend Who Never Picks Up the Check
Every student of literature knows that Kit Marlowe was stabbed to death as he sat drinking with three companions in a tavern in Deptford, England. Did you ever wonder why?

To True Lovers Who Lament the Fact That They Cannot Live Forever
You already have.

To One Who Won't Get Over It

You seem awfully fragile for the weight of a grudge. It might be the one thing you're not able to bear.

To My Favorite Satirist

You are like the washroom in a church—out of place and indispensable.

To a Young Artist Who Searches for a Brand-new Subject

Don't.

On the Noblesse of Women

It goes way back. Even Adam was exonerated.

On Bloodsuckers

Should a vampire require a transfusion, and it is your blood type, and yours alone, that will save his life, ask yourself: How many ways should you give blood to a vampire?

To a Critic Whose Work Has Come to Nothing

Why? you ask. Because you cannot tell flippancy from sorrow. Simple.

To Those Who Say That They Have Learned from
Past Mistakes
    Very good. That's a good one. I like that.

To One Who Has the Power to Cause Harm
    You call that power?

To One Who Catches My Drift
    Thanks. It's all I've got—drift.

The Albatross That Brought Everyone Good Luck

—✐—

I should write a fable about an albatross that brings everyone good luck, wonderful luck; or one about a sword belonging to someone named Damocles, Tom Damocles, that liberates its owner and smites evildoers; or one about a wolf in sheep's clothing who is simply a cross-dresser, quite harmless; or one about a last straw that turns to gold and turns all the other straws to gold and makes the recipient rich.

But I will not do that, of course. One must retain one's standard metaphors, or else how will one be able to sidestep the truth?

Bring a Wildebeest Home
to Mother

—w—

At first she will be appalled. She will ask you: "Where did you get that wildebeest?" And she will tell you: "Take it back at once!" However, you will find that if you do not take the wildebeest back at once, but rather say nothing and let the animal stay for the evening, your mother will begin to grow accustomed to the animal, which you have now named Chip. By the following morning, in spite of the chaos created (crushed chairs, smashed china), she, too, is calling it Chip.

Next, bring home a baby tiger and see what happens. Once again, your mother will be appalled, and aghast as well, and she will say: "A wildebeest is one thing, a tiger another." But here, too, if you keep your wits about you and let things happen as they will, Lucky the tiger will soon be part of the family—though one day you may find that Chip has disappeared.

In a little while, bring home a full-grown elephant.

You *did* ask how demagogues were born?

Jaws's Side of Things

You try eating while people are batting you over the head with oars and splashing about and taking shots at you with a .357 Magnum. Someone even tried to blow me up with dynamite. See how *you'd* like it. If you ask me (of course, you won't), the trouble with the world today is that no one lets you do what you do best. There's always somebody out there ready with a new and different direction, the suggestion of a hobby, perhaps. What would I do, I'd like to know? Collect stamps?

Look. I eat. That's my name and that's my game. Or, to be more accurate, *you're* my game. Too bad for you. And, if I say so myself, I'm pretty good at my specialty—a virtuoso. My friends call me that.

What did you expect, may I ask? That I would slink away, repent, or better still, reform? If only you could see yourselves—so hot and bothered on the shore, so vengeful, so warlike (I'm impressed), and oh, so sorry that I am what I am and not sitting limp in a decorative glass cup, with sauce on the side, like some dumb-ass shrimp cocktail.

Dogstoevsky

—⁓—

The dog. By Roger Rosenblatt. The dog barks. By Roger Rosenblatt. The dog barks by Roger Rosenblatt who is trying to read *Crime and Punishment* by Fyodor Dostoevsky. He is trying to read *Crime and Punishment* by Fyodor Dostoevsky, but the dog barks. As Raskolnikov dodges his landlady, the dog barks. As Raskolnikov curses his sister's fate, the dog barks, too. The dog always barks. By Rodya Raskolnikov. *Dogs and Punishment* by Rodya Rosenblatt, by Roger Raskolnikov, by Fyodog Dogstoevsky. Barkbarkbarkbarkbark.

I am not crazy yet. The dog has not barked me to craziness quite yet. All I have sought to do for the past two days, sitting in the same chair in the same house with the same Hershey's Kisses left over from Halloween at my same left hand; all I have sought is to make some progress with *Crime and Punishment,* and so I have considered killing the dog, as Raskolnikov killed the two old women.

If you kill one dog, after all, what does it matter to the balance of the world, if you know what I mean, and I think you do.

Of course, you do not hear the barking; you, swaddled in the sweet silence of your Ford Taurus or your Library of Congress, you do not hear my cairn terrier with the tommy-gun voice. Nor can you hear what my cairn terrier hears. Nor can I. But I can hear her. It is a metaphysical riddle, is it not, that she barks at what she hears, but I can only hear her barking. Who then would hear the sound if I felled her with a tree in the forest? Bark to bark.

What gets me is how little she cares for my peace of mind. She has not read *Crime and Punishment*. She knows nothing of the pleasures of sitting back with Hershey's Kisses on a dismal November afternoon— the trees shorn, the wind mixing with rain—and reading of starving young Russians tormenting themselves in the city of ———, in the year ———. Six long years I have owned this dog, feeding and bathing and tummy-scratching in return for puppy barking and dog barking. She is not six, I remind her. She is forty-two. Time to settle down, I remind her. *Tempus fugit. Cave canem.* (Barkbarkbark.) She is not the dog I had hoped for, not that dog at all.

Not that I was hoping for Lassie, if that's what you're thinking. Or Rin Tin Tin, or Yukon King, or Fala, or Checkers, or Him, or Her, or a dog that flies or takes fingerprints or says "Ruth" in bars. I was not expecting Ms. Magic Dog of the Twenty-First Century, who could not only fetch my copy of *Crime and Punishment*, but who could also have translated the book from the original. Not my dog. Not the dog of my dreams.

All I ever wanted was a good and quiet dog, like the dignified hound in Piero di Cosimo's *Death of Procris*, sitting so mournfully, so nobly at the feet of his fallen master. A dog like that would not bark more than once a month (once in his seven). A dog like that would know his place in the order of things and would state by the mere fact of his docile existence that there are those who rule and those who sit quietly, those who read *Crime and Punishment* and those who don't, and therefore do not make it impossible for those who do, just because they hear things that those who do, don't.

Barkbarkbarkbarkbark.

There is nothing out there. I have been stalled on page 71 for an hour, and there is nothing out there. Raskolnikov has axed the two old women over and over again. He feels no remorse. He is consumed with purpose. He can do whatever he wants to do—sans guilt, sans cairns—he for whom no dog barks.

Now she is still for a moment. The brown, blank eyes fixed with alarm. The head loaded, ready to fire. What can she hear? Is it the sound of an enemy I cannot hear yet? Or is it the sound of the enemy I can never hear, the sound of evil itself, of my own murderous impulse to kill the very dog who barks to keep me from killing the very dog who barks to keep me from killing me?

Love Song

—*m*—

If those pushy mothers of the Plaza de Mayo, years ago in Argentina, didn't go away no matter how the *policia* shoved them around; if they continued to walk up and down in front of the presidential Pink House carrying photographs on placards and holding snapshots between their index fingers and their thumbs; if they insisted day after day, sunshine or rain, that their children did indeed exist in spite of the fact that they had been "disappeared" by the thugs of the military government, proving by their dogged persistence that there was no such thing as a *desaparecido* or that nothing beloved could vanish just like that . . . why would you think that I might disappear?

Go Where You Are Loved

—✥—

Go where you are loved, and where you love. But you, being you, will, of course, make the other choice and head off for enemy quarters where you will be greeted by handshakes, chocolates, and flowers. There, people will tell you how splendid you look, how beautiful your mind is, while, out of your sight, they will plot your assassination. At night you sleep without dreams and curl a stupid smile on your stupid face.

As for those you love and who love you, you have persuaded yourself that they can wait. The remarkable thing is that they will.

Essays. I, Too, Dislike Them

—⁓—

The essay consists of one part poetry, two parts history, three parts philosophy, and no parts sex.

My point of entry is a young woman standing before you reading a book, waiting for a train. She wears a round straw hat girded by a thick blue band. Her sandals are open-toed. Her dress is white with a pattern of small yellow flowers. Her skirt stops at her knees. Her expression skitters between the quizzical and the serene. She never lifts her gaze from the pages of the book, and she shows no concern for the time, the station, the train, her eventual destination, or for you.

What do you think? Is she a vision from a painting by Degas? Is she Galatea? Is she the intersection of thought and space? A problem? A symbol? A doop doop de doop?

Is that bulge in your pants a thousand words long?

If in My Sleep

If, in my sleep, I shout unintelligible names or indicate anguish in a garbled tongue, or call out in horror or surprise, or utter a lament in Spanish, though I do not know Spanish, or laugh—laugh wildly—you may be sure that I am dreaming of a black glass wall with tall, cracked ladders leaning against it, and I am clambering up the side, only to find that I am crawling on the ceiling of a tunnel, and below me are red horses in stampede—dreaming, that is, of my life as an impossible puzzle.

So please do not push or nudge or tap or make any effort to get me up, for I fear that I may wake into sleep and understand everything.

Instructions to the Housekeeper

—⁓—

Please wash the sheets and polish the silver. Please dust the piano, do the shopping, and cook dinner. Please fix the lamp in the hall and the sprinkler system. Please rebuild car engine (the Lexus). Please point up the bricks on the west wall of the house and relay the foundation (steel beams to replace locust posts). Please stop teenagers from getting tattoos. Please explain to said teens that rifts always occur between parents and children and that everything will be all right. Please make life more pleasant for me at work and give Brooks an injury that forces him to stay home for several months. Please add a little spice to my marriage—sex, culture, etc. I'm concerned about the market—please improve. Cure cancer, end world hunger, terrorism, and so forth. Racism, ditto. Thank you.

P.S. Please do the shirts right this time. No starch.

"Neglect"

Naturally, you called it "neglect," and it was neglect—
the absence of attention, the omission of attention—
as when a town in which an industry once thrived (a
steel mill or a shoe factory) is fallen from neglect, and
the eaves of the roofs sag soaked with rain, the door of
the bank vault lies open to houseflies, the grocer's
shelves are thick with dust, the druggist's shelves the
same. And nothing remains of the school yard except
a jungle gym in a heap of pipes and a chain-link fence
that has been yanked from its stanchions. Still, you
were right. Technically, it was neglect. Don't give it a
second thought.

With Narcissus in the Aquarium

—⁓—

"I can't see my reflection for the fish," he said. He was wearing a white silk shirt from Paris, a Zegna tie, and a suit custom made in heaven.

"That's the point," I told him. "Look at these beauties."

I showed him the larvaceans weaving their mucous nets, and the comb jellies and the barrel-shaped salps. I showed him a thirty-foot siphonophore and noted how these creatures did not have advanced nervous systems, or brains, or eyes, and were nonetheless able to defend themselves and hunt. I showed him the chambered nautilus and the octopus, and the cuttlefish that disappear in smoke of their own making.

"Look there," I said. And I showed him the shovel-nose guitarfish and a grouper rowing by using its pectorals as oars. I tried to engage his interest in the synchronized swimming of the silver sardines and the schools of mackerel gleaming in the light. But I could see that he didn't care, didn't care for any of it.

Then suddenly he stopped. He stared at one of the glass cases. He lay down his briefcase containing his schedule of lectures and his schedule of TV appearances and a list of the phone calls he had to return from important people in Washington and New York.

What enthralled him was the *Vampyroteuthis infernalis,* the vampire squid from hell, with its salmon-colored body that can hide in the cloak of itself, its salmon-colored head, and its blue eye—that blue eye of the *Vampyroteuthis infernalis,* which is no ordinary blue, but the blue of the first blue ever, the blue that defines the color, the blue open eye of the sea itself.

"You know," he said at last. "That eye. That eye."

"What about it?" I asked.

"It's looking at me."

Kilroy Was Here

—⁓—

Every place in World War II, every foxhole, every tank, every available surface displayed the mystifying graffiti KILROY WAS HERE. A riddle. A joke. For decades, people asked, "Who's Kilroy?"—as if that were the question.

Tell me a story. Tell me a story about Kilroy and *why* he was here. Tell me about you being here and about me being here. Oh, yes. And about Jean-Dominique Bauby, the editor-in-chief of the French edition of *Elle,* who suffered so massive a stroke that the only part of his body he could move was his left eyelid. So, with that left eyelid he signaled the alphabet—*a, b, c*—to others, and thus was able to write a whole book, a bestseller. He used his eyelid to write a book: *The Diving Bell and the Butterfly.* He, too, was here. *Ici.*

Along with the Jews of the Warsaw Ghetto who, in their final days, after they had watched their mothers and cousins shoved off to the extermination camps in the dead of winter and were themselves at the edge of death from diphtheria and malnutrition, still they took little pieces of paper and rolled them up in scrolls and wrote things on them—poems, fragments of autobiography, political tracts—and slipped the scrolls into the crevices of the ghetto walls.

Which acts would have been perfectly understood by Chekhov's horse, to whom the narrator of Chekhov's story told of his little boy's death because there was no one else to tell his story to. Neigh?

Why did they bother, you know? You know.

For the same reason the ancient mariner, crazy as a loon, grabbed the wedding guest by the lapels and would not let go until ... for the same reason that the messenger in Job says: "And I only am escaped alone to tell thee." To *tell* thee. Which was Ishmael's reason, too, practically word for word.

You know. You know. They had a story to tell. They had to tell a story, which is why you are here and I am here. Sing it: "We're here because we're here because we're here because we're here."

And Kilroy, the very-short-story writer? Well, you certainly know why he was here.

The Puppet Theater
of Your Irrational Fears

—*m*—

has the twisted pleasure of presenting: "Your Friend Hasn't Called in Two Weeks." Plus: "You Discover a Dead Crow on Your Lawn." In Theater 2: "Someone Tells You That You're in for a Big Surprise." And: "Letters Received Written in Pencil with No Return Address." Coming soon: "R.S.V.P. We're Having an Intimate Dinner Party—Just Eight or Ten of Us." And: "Dawn."

Teach the Free Man
How to Praise

—⁓—

I never got that line until I'd lived a little. "Teach the free man how to praise." It comes from Auden's elegy to Yeats, and one has to slow down at "free" to understand the whole thought. The free man is free to do everything, which is the nature of his freedom. So he is free to moan, rail, and curse; and this is what he does most often. But he is also free to praise. He may use his freedom to give praise.

These ducks, for example, that whet out in arrowhead formations over the Atlantic. And the Atlantic herself that gushes in the half-light after a hard rain. And the beach that contorts to shapes of angels on tombstones, awls, hunchbacks, lovers lying thigh to thigh. And the driftwood from a mackerel schooner that still bears the stench of the catch. And the slant of the sky. And the shingles of the sky. And a cloud like Tennessee. And the face of our dog—ill, old, uncomplaining dog.

And you, with your Welsh courage and your girl's profile and your tireless sense of me. Did I mention you? *Ave.*

The Day I Turned into
the Westin

—⁓—

Fortunately, on the day I turned into the Westin, it was still early enough to allow me to prepare for the onslaught of guests. My brain, which had become the lobby-level bar and grill, began to cook the home fries and open-face steak sandwiches, a favorite with the afterhours crowd; and the piano player, my left ear, though hungover from the previous night and slumped atop a D-seventh, had plenty of time to straighten up and fly right. My wrists, the bellhops, donned their red uniforms with the brass buttons and got the baggage carts ready. My knees, the swimming pool and spa, made certain that all was spic and span and that the towels, my eyelashes, were nice and hot.

In the pit of my stomach, which was the terrace lounge for the higher-paying guests, I wondered if my nose, the housekeeping staff, could get up to speed in so short a time. I had, after all, just turned into the Westin that morning. I wondered the same thing about my right elbow, which was room service, and my lower back, maintenance and security. It takes constant vigilance to be a hotel. Much coordination. When the guests emerge from the revolving doors, my index finger and thumb, they expect everything to be shipshape, which is why my Adam's apple, the escalator, is developing a case of nerves.

How I became the Westin, I cannot say. But I was not always like this. My heart, the concierge, would like to inform the guests that not all that long ago, say twenty-five or thirty years, I might have been taken for the Grand Hotel Villa Serbelloni with its high burnt-ochre walls that stretched to twenty-four-foot ceilings, with playful cupids painted on them, and with the enormous open windows cut in stone that looked out upon the gardens where the German nannies watched over children of false nobility and out upon Lake Como and the Villa Serbelloni itself, once the home of Pliny the Younger—the blue, still shell of the lake and the orange-tile roofs beyond and beyond that, the snowy Alps. To be sure, I was not really the Grand Hotel Villa Serbelloni, but I might have passed. In any case, I was certainly classier than I am now. First class. Ask anyone.

Chaucer slept here. And Shakespeare. Donne and

Marvell dropped by the tavern, my liver, more than once; and Milton, though he needed the help of strangers, would stroll around the ballroom and hear the tinkling of the vast crystal chandelier, my throat. Swift, Pope, Johnson, they all knew my place and would regularly book rooms in my tongue for a night or two. In later years, Jane Austen took an apartment in my ribs, and when George Eliot saw how comfortable Jane was, she did the same. Musicians, painters, philosophers—they all thought of me as their home away from home. You should have seen the silverware in those days, how heavy it felt in one's hands. And the thick, cool linens.

Now look at me. It's not that I have anything against the Westin I've turned into. I could have become a Marriott, I suppose, or a Hyatt, or a Hilton, and not felt any different. I'm no Motel 6—not yet. No complaints. Fact is, I'm not sure how I became a hotel in the first place, because I can remember way back—long before the Villa Serbelloni days—when I thought of myself as a guest, as one for whom all services were created. But then one day I found myself making accommodations, small ones at first, then more ample, more elaborate, until...ah, well. *C'est la guerre,* as they say. And, frankly, there is simply too much for me to do to worry about where life took a detour or any such self-indulgence. Only I wish that there weren't quite so much upkeep when one is a hotel these days. People expect everything.

I'm thinking of changing my toes, the pizzeria, into a Japanese restaurant; everyone is crazy for sushi. My feet are working on becoming trainers for the gym. Hands, masseurs; lips, a hotel playroom for kids. A kennel, even, in my right thigh. They take their dogs everywhere.

Sometimes at night, when my lungs, the registration desk, have stopped throbbing from anxiety, I wander about my jaws, the kitchen, and dream of being something else. But then night softens into day, another day, and there are all the guests' demands to attend to. They complain that they are unable to turn off the clock-radios in their rooms. They want square, not round, chocolate mints on their pillows. The most difficult part will come not when I have shaved my awning face or brushed my elevator-bank teeth, or even tied my tie around my WELCOME TO THE WESTIN sign, my neck. It will be when I begin to smile my smile, which has become my smile.

Cliff's Other Notes

—m—

Cyrano

Don't for a moment believe that it was Cyrano's nose. Anyone can see that it wasn't his nose. Women actually found it alluring, kind of sexy. But he deluded himself and blamed the nose. If only someone, Roxanne, for example, had told him the truth—that what women could not take was his ardor, his passion, the overflowing vessel of his heart. It was too much. They found it—what?—grotesque. So he hid in the shadows to speak his oversized heart, when it was the heart itself that scared them off.

Dr. Jekyll and Mr. Hyde

It has to be about drugs. Jekyll is a junkie. Right?

Gatsby

If you hold *The Great Gatsby* upside down and

shake it hard enough, the only real human being who falls out is Wilson the garageman. Gatsby is obsessed to the point of madness. Daisy is a dangerous nitwit. Tom is a thug, Jordan a crook, Meyer (though decent) a gangster. Even Nick, for all his moralizing, is mere talk, and not even that when it counts. Only the poor deceived Wilson is identifiable as one of us suffering slobs. So what is Fitzgerald saying by this—that one does not make memorable fiction out of ordinary suffering slobs? That no one would read *The Great Wilson*? I think so.

Dorian

The lesson of *The Picture of Dorian Gray* is thought to involve inner corruption as opposed to outer appearance. But the lesson is more easily learned without reference to the aging portrait. Look at Dorian as he is—forever youthful, pretty, and unwrinkled. He is living proof that if one thinks of oneself throughout one's life, one may go on and on without showing the faintest signs of aging. Eternal youth is thus another name for perpetual selfishness. I wouldn't worry about the attic, if I were you.

Ulysses

Everyone who followed Homer minced words about *Ulysses,* including Dante. All of them pussy-footed around the story, which seems to me to be as plain as daylight. What made Ulysses's eye rove, along with the rest of him, was the irresistible attraction of doing the wrong thing—of doing it again and again, and knowing that he was doing the wrong thing. It shows what a good man Dante was that he could not bring himself to say that outright.

The Secret Agent

There's a scene in Conrad's novel that merely appears to be part of the plot, but I think that it explains everything one needs to know about Verloc, the anarchist. Verloc is lying on the couch. His wife is in the kitchen. She has just figured out that he is responsible for the death by bomb of her young son. She gets a kitchen knife and heads for Verloc. Conrad describes the scene by telling us that Verloc has time to see her, time to see her get the knife, and time to see her walk toward him; but he does not have time to do anything about it. That's Verloc, and all anarchists. They have no sense of time.

Sir Gawain and the Green Knight, "Kubla Khan,"
A Christmas Carol, Moby-Dick, The Maltese Falcon,
For Whom the Bell Tolls, Remembrance of Things Past
(all eight books), *The Wasteland,* "September 1,
1939," *and Hamlet*

All these works have their moments, but not one
of them makes an ounce of sense—especially *Hamlet*.
For God's sake, *Goldilocks and the Three Bears* makes
more sense than *Hamlet*. I just wanted to get that off
my chest.

Environmentalists

—✦—

I have often been in this spot, and of recent years I have felt that this might be the last time that I should look down from here upon the kingdom of the world and their glories; but see, it happened once again, and I hope that even this is not the last time that we shall both spend a pleasant day here. In future we must often come up here.

That was Goethe to his friend, Eckermann, on September 26, 1827, as the two men sat on the grass and had a picnic at Buchenwald.

Hearing Test

—*m*—

Can you hear this?
Sounds like church bells, people laughing, glasses clinking.

Can you hear this?
What? The baby's cry? Yes, I can hear it.

Can you hear this?
A door slamming, I think. And china breaking.

Can you hear this?
It's faint. I can barely make it out. It sounds like the wearing away of the inside of a tunnel or a universal joint or maybe the underside of ice on a frozen pond. Something eroding out of sight, from the side one cannot see. But I can't be certain.

Very good. That's exactly what it was.

Everywhere a Hit Person

—◦◦◦—

Friends sometimes ask me why I am aloof with people. I tell them I have learned that a hit man (or woman) has been hired to bump me off. I do not know who did the hiring; and, of course, I have no inkling as to the identity of the hit person. It could be anyone, I say. Not all hit people are as attractive as Kathleen Turner or Angelica Huston in the movies. Or as appealing as John Cusack or William H. Macy. My hit person could be the grouchy redhead in the laundromat, or the Korean Fuller Brush representative at my door, or the pet-store manager, the one with the lisp who has difficulty pronouncing "marsupial." Any one of these people could be the person hired to do me in, along with a thousand others I have yet to meet.

And, I explain, because I have no way of knowing who that person might be, it is only prudent for me to keep my distance as a general practice.

They usually stop asking after that.

Lessons for Grades 1 to 6

—*m*—

About Language

Soon enough, you'll find English to be inadequate for your needs. Make up your own language and be sure not to know the meaning of the words you make up. A language of your own will keep grown-ups at a distance. They'll call it cute. Flarto.

About Money

It may not be everything. But remember that the tragedy of every Irish play could be solved or prevented by eight or nine pounds.

About Political Correctness

It's okay to demonize demons. That's what they're here for.

About Thinking

Up to a point, it's fine. This point is where your

thought comes to a pause and you feel compelled to extend it, as if you are walking through a rain forest in Suriname and you have come to a log of a bridge and you have the choice of either walking over the bridge on your march through the forest or stopping in your tracks and feeling the sweet, wet heat of the sun on your arms. Nothing more than that. The sweet, wet heat of the sun on your arms.

About Plato

He said, "Light is the shadow of God." I'm not sure what it means, either. But try to recognize a superior mind when you meet it.

About the Shapes of Things

Socrates spoke of the beauty of shapes "quite free from the itch of desire." That's a very intelligent thing to say. Very high-minded. But know, too, that your urge to scratch did not appear from nowhere.

About Animals

A friend I made in Ireland many years ago—much older than I, full of poetry and mischief, and a good Catholic as well—had known James Joyce in his last years. He said that Joyce could not abide his darker side, his baser behavior, his low and dirty thoughts. "We're all animals," my friend told him. But Joyce, he said, would not accept that.

About Face

Make two pictures of yourself—a photo and a portrait. Be sure they are as good as they can be. The photo catches you in the most flattering light. The portrait, less precise, shows the hazier but deeper you. Place them side by side and, once in a while (not every day), study them, first one, then the other. Then study the space between the pictures. Somewhere in that space, you exist. That's you. That's your face.

About Being Scared

Since nothing in life can go on without the wind, I wouldn't worry about trembling if I were you.

About Writing

If you have to do it, do it. But do it because you have to. Not because you think it will cure your sciatica.

About Latin

Learn it.

About Obstinacy

The trouble with hardening one's heart (as God discovered when he was toying with Pharaoh) is not that the heart turns to stone, but that stone endures.

About the Body

Trust it. Keats wrote of his beloved Fanny Brawne: "Everything that reminds me of her goes through me like a spear."

About ADD

It's bad for you. Everyone says so. But without it, how else will you get in the car one day, all by yourself, and without any advance warning, and without telling a soul, drive to Mexico?

About Your Conscience

It, too, can lie.

If You Had Given It
a Moment's Thought

—⁕—

If you had given it a moment's thought, you might not have made that lame joke about dying to a cancer patient. But you didn't think, of course. Just like you. This happens to you more often than it should. Then you think: Life's like this—a perpetual pursuit of small satisfactions such as being funny, or being charming, or being anything. Nickle-and-dime decisions, and yet the repercussions are often bedlam. Chaos without the theory.

I wish that I could tell you how to stop. But frankly, the consequences of one's little stumbles get so tumultuous sometimes that one's amazement at them overtakes the desire for self-improvement. So you go on as before. An ice storm comes to mind. The interesting thing about an ice storm is that it isn't defined until it's over. Then you see the ice.

The Bathroom for You

—m—

Today's bathroom is more than a sink, tub, and a toilet. It's a personal space where you can retreat from the stresses of everyday life.

—Home magazine

The bathroom for you will have more than a sink, tub, and a toilet. It will have a walk-in shower made of the finest Belgian marble. The floor will be of Mexican tile to give the room that expansive feel of the American Southwest, and the lighting fixtures will be recessed and attached to a dimmer, which will allow you to change the room's moods, brighter or darker, according to your own, and will allow you to retreat from the stresses of everyday life.

The bathroom for you will have a patio and a swimming pool, with little jets built into its side to create the effect of a whirlpool. In another part of the room, there will be armchairs and a sofa to offer a place where you can stretch out and relax. You will also have a large-screen TV that gets 212 movie channels, each playing your favorite movies, and a wet bar, in case you get wet (ha ha). Don't confuse the walk-in closets with the walk-in shower. Just kidding.

The bathroom for you will look out on the Atlantic Ocean to the south and on the Grand Tetons to the west. There will be a separate guest cottage for guests, and an artist's studio for art. It will also contain your own office tower that rises over a hundred stories, and which you alone occupy, except for the shops that are there to satisfy your every need—more drains, more faucets, and so forth. In your tower you will be CEO, so that if you wish to cash in on stock options before you go under, feel free.

We can hear you ask: "Who's going to pay for all this?" The bathroom for you includes your very own bank, which will provide all the funds you ever require, and your very own stock exchange, where your stocks only go up up up. You will never "take a bath" (ha ha).

The bathroom for you will be both city and country. It will include over fifty square hectares of fields, where you can grow oats and wheat and barley. Plenty of room for tractors and combines. And should an accident occur (God forbid!) you will have a fully equipped hospital, with several operating theaters and nurses on strike, to add that touch of realism. To further ensure your privacy, as well as your protection, there will be a fleet of planes on hand, outfitted with both short- and long-range missiles (nuclear, natch), in case of an invasion from another bathroom. Just kidding.

The bathroom for you is infinitely expandable, so if there is anything we have left out—baseball and football stadiums, movie theaters, concert halls, museums, a petting zoo for your pets—the omission is easily remedied. Many of our customers are cautious by nature, so we have added your personal law firm and your own courthouse, including an appellate division, in case you slip in the tub and feel like suing yourself (ha ha).

The bathroom for you means personal freedom, we realize that. So we will include a desert island; we call it "Your Escape Within an Escape." On the island will be all the things one needs in a state of seclusion—books on self-improvement, books on self-recrimination, and, naturally, a bathroom.

At the same time, the bathroom for you may begin to feel too private, too enclosed, and you may feel guilty that you have focused all this attention on your bathroom, while so much of the outer world is starving or dying of disease. We know how you feel, so we have added most of Asia, all of Africa, and underclass America to your bathroom, along with medical researchers to find cures for the ill and captains of industry to provide meaningful work for the poor. As for those who still remain hostile after all that, who indeed may seek to eradicate you and your bathroom—we can see you begin to smile already—yes! We have provided them with bathrooms, too.

In preparing the bathroom for you we have tried to think of everything, but we also realize that inevitably there will be items we could not have anticipated. So, just in case, we have added an architectural firm to make any additions or corrections you require to make this room uniquely yours. The only thing that matters is that you feel totally comfortable and that you achieve the peace of mind that says: This room is you. One thing we do ask is that you keep the shower curtain inside the shower and that you don't forget to flush. Just kidding.

13 Ways of Looking
at a Blackboard

—◆—

1. A manic syntax of desks and chairs; a lost syntax of knowledge and feeling; and the day the fat lady with the blue hair and nothing under it demanded that I spell the word *syntax,* and I guessed right, not because I was smart or clever, but because I knew that, more than anything, she wanted me to get it wrong.

2. You Mean to Say You Didn't Learn a Thing? Long division, as long as it was not too long. The spelling of *recommend*. The poem, "Musée des Beaux Arts" and the proper pronunciation of Brueghel. And, speaking of that, the location of Auden's house on St. Mark's Place, where I would go instead of class in the afternoons and stand across the street from his apartment

and stare up. I could take you there if you like.

3. Today's Math and Science Questions:
   1. If every equation balances out; that is, if both sides always come to the same thing, why are we forcing you to take math?
   2. Except for the language of science, there is hardly a word that has but a single meaning. (Same question as math.)

4. Wallace Stevens said that in the long run the truth does not matter. Lucky for us, because we certainly didn't learn the truth. We learned that art is long but life is short, and that certainly wasn't true. Come to think of it, I can't recall a single thing I learned that was true. One thing, maybe. On the wall next to my desk in a classroom in the basement, a prior lifer had written, very neatly, "Mushy mounds of Mongolian moose manure." That was true.

5. Read *The Forsythe Saga* by Thursday.

6. History—F

   Algebra—F

   French—F

   Desire to Make Friends—F

   Desire to Open a Book—F

   Desire to Do Anything But Write Poems and Shoot Baskets—F

   Belief in Self in Spite of Everything We've Done—A (See below.)

   > We are very concerned about his performance in this class. We have done everything imaginable to smash his self-confidence, and yet he persists in feeling that he can make something of his life. Please schedule a conference immediately.

7. Club Meetings for the Week: The Treachery Society; Malice and Gossip Team; Psycho Boys (aka Future Psychologists of America); Cowed, Lonely, and Scared People (CLASP)—please bring nicknames; Also, tryouts in the theater for major parts in *Othello, The Bad Seed, All About Eve, Carrie.*

8. It was no more than a glimpse from one of the high, rippling windows of the Meeting House. A tree tilting in the playground. A daffodil poking up between two slabs of slate. A guillotine of morning light descending on a wall of old red brick. The picture could have been anywhere beautiful—the home of a great artist, a museum, a monastery, a school.

9. Mr. McGrath, from the zoo, who has taken the claws out of animals, will speak at assembly this Tuesday. Bring your pets.

10. From the principal's office: As you know, we have admitted one black student in the 150-year history of the school, and we admitted that one just yesterday. When he arrives, I trust that you will give him the school welcome and treat him as you would one another.

11. P.S. Whoever wrote the following under "anonymous" in the yearbook, see me at once: "The Greeks say that we have death

with us every step of our lives, so that when we finally die, we already know what death is. I cannot speak for my classmates. But I for one would like to thank the school for teaching me about the Greeks."

12. Fucking up our lives was merely their way; they meant no harm. Or, to be accurate, they meant no more harm to us than they did to anyone else. In their previous lives they might have been people. Our luck! The drunk who taught chemistry and who was rumored to have been gassed in the war, which accounted, they said, for our inability to understand a syllable he uttered; the one who taught biology and theorized that if a fat man married a skinny woman, they would have an ordinary-size child; the baseball coach who called me a kike because I'd walked a man with the bases loaded and who claimed to have played in the majors under a different name, but hadn't; the wobbly married couple who taught math and bounced off each other

like zeppelins making private, incomprehensible jokes; the one who threw bric-a-brac at the kids; the one who fed us sugar cubes (he was one of the nicest); the harridan who taught French so that she could make students feel like dirt in two languages. That was the quality of the faculty.

All except Shank, who came from the Mormons by way of Yale and taught us how to read a poem and how to think of writing as a selection of exact words; who gave us passages of poetry with a key word missing and had us fill in the blanks; who gave us Canada Mints and asked us to write what they tasted like, to teach us metaphor; who began our study of *Hamlet* by having us build a model of the Globe Theatre; who had standards and who was gay and who was fired because of both defects. They called him a homo. He was.

13. SECOND GRADERS—DO NOT ERASE! "Every day in every way I'm getting better and better."

Something's Wrong

You have that look on your face. You don't need a mirror. You can feel the squint of anguished curiosity, the formation of a poorly drawn set of quotation marks between your eyebrows, the absentminded, kind of dumb, pucker of the lips. Absentmindedness. That could be it. The location of the car keys, the sunglasses. Perhaps that's what's on your mind. Something is wrong, that's for sure. Perhaps you can't find a ballpoint pen. You must buy a billion of those pens every year, and they all disappear. Perhaps you can't recall the name of Max Von Sydow. You stared at his face for a full hour as you watched the movie, *Minority Report,* knowing that you'd seen that face before, a long time ago, in Ingmar Bergman movies.

You could be worried about that. You could be worried about forgetfulness in general, about the next time you see Max Von Sydow on the screen and having to wait until the credits roll in the blackness before his name comes to you. Something's wrong. Something's clearly wrong. If not that, this. If not this, then something else.

Perhaps it's your money. Plenty of reason to be concerned about money these days. Your investments. Could be that. Your investment house. Could be a bunch of crooks. So could your bank. So many crooks in big business, these days. Is that what's behind your malaise? Malaise: Maybe it's your body. The body is supposed to send signals when it's in trouble, but some of the most serious diseases don't send any signals, none that we recognize. Is it your aorta, colon, spleen? Perhaps you don't know your ass from your elbow. Time to learn?

Perhaps you're merely tired, pooped, bushed, and a benumbing weariness has fooled you into thinking that something's wrong. Then again, you may be going mad. Some of the best people do, you know. The phone rang once this morning, only once, and you wondered for quite a while why someone had hung up after just one ring. What possibly could have occurred to make someone do that? Had the call come from a car? Perhaps the car had been in an accident, gouged from behind by an oil truck, and both vehicles were sent plunging in a loop-the-loop of fire down a ravine into a lake.

Had the phone call come from someone you hadn't seen in decades, since high school, who suddenly acted on an impulse, but then, after a single ring, thought the better of it and returned to her job as a waitress at Appleby's? Was it Mary Baker Eddy, calling from her cool tomb? Why did she pick *you*? But she must have regretted her choice. She hung up.

It could be worse, of course. What's wrong could be a lie you told, a wrong you committed, or a right you omitted to commit. People do that, too. They fail to correct a false impression someone has of a friend of theirs, they fail to stand up for their loved ones, they maintain a self-protective silence when a good word would have been the right thing to say. They agree with disagreeable ideas. It has happened. That injury you caused so many years ago, is it still getting you down? Why, the injured party has probably forgotten the incident. Why bring it up now? Unless it is the thing that's wrong.

Something's wrong, all right. You just can't put your finger on it. Maybe it's the position of the planets. Saturn's rings could be dipping a degree or two.

Or something you're picking out of the air—a lounge singer, perhaps, sad-eyed in a tight yellow dress, standing beside a Yamaha baby grand in the Hyatt in Saipan and murmuring, "Am I Blue?" just a shade off-key, every note just a shade off-key—something like that could turn the trick. Or the way the fates operate. On the news you heard about a woman in Hawaii who was killed when a four-ton boulder broke loose, rolled down a mountain, and crashed through the wall of her home into her bedroom where she had been sleeping and crushed her to death. What are the odds of something like that happening? Enough to drive you to distraction, and you certainly are distracted.

Whatever it is, you know it's important. Might even have been fundamental, indispensable to your well-being. Like an appointment missed that might have changed everything. Something you neglected to do, to follow up on, to say that could have made you happy forever. The day you failed to seize. The person you neglected to speak to. The love that was there for the taking. The life that was there for the taking. But you settled, didn't you? You let it stroll right past you, didn't you? Is that it? Is that it? Yes, yes. That's it. That's it. No, that isn't it.

Shorter than Bacon's (More)

On Bigotry

You think it has to do with race and religion, but it goes much wider. The one who believes only in his own point of view is a fine old bigot.

On Blushes

They come to the surface when one is either modest or ashamed. Interesting, no?

On Doubt

Doubt is the mother (or father) of belief. And vice versa. I have no idea where that gets you.

On Cheats

It figures: One who hides behind a cheat has to be smaller than the cheat.

On Murderers

On the whole, they're better than liars. And a half-murder is a lot better than a half-truth.

On Being Without Love

If no one, absolutely no one, loves you, you're doing something wrong. Bet on it.

The Giant Rat of Sumatra

—*m*—

For much of my youth, my ambitions centered on lines from movies. There were certain things said in movies that I cherished—things that I knew that I wanted to hear again and again. I sought to incorporate them into my life, which is to say that I wanted to work them into normal conversations. Friends would be conducting a perfectly sensible chat, and I would be listening, like a lion in the brush, for an opportunity to slip in a line from, say, *Beau Brummel* ("Who's your fat friend?") or *Double Indemnity* ("There's a widespread feeling that just because a man has a large office, he must be an idiot") or *Palm Beach Story* (as said by Rudy Vallee to Mary Astor: "You know, Maude, someone meeting you for the first time, not knowing you were cracked, might get the wrong impression of you." For that one, of course, one would have to wait for someone named Maude).

To be sure, this hobby of mine did not make me the ideal social companion, but this is how it is when career and popularity are in conflict. The "fat friend" line earned me the everlasting hatred of a plumpish girl in high school, who was standing beside a friend of mine when I tossed in my movie question. I tried to explain that I was merely quoting Stewart Granger as Beau Brummel when he was miffed with King George III, but she seemed uninterested.

The lines I chose were never the garden variety, such as "Louis, I think this is the beginning of a beautiful friendship" or "Frankly, my dear..." and so forth, but rather ones that had a special attraction for me. The other day I heard such a line in a movie called *Jack Frost,* in which someone who was attempting to rid the world of a large maniacal snowman, explained: "We tried blowing him up, but it only pissed him off."

For many years, there were two lines I had never been able to slip into any conversation. The first of these, I never did get in. It occurred in *Earthquake,* one of the disaster films of the 1970s, in which a man was stalking a young woman to do terrible things to her. One would have thought that an earthquake would have been enough to divert his attention, but he was determined. At the height of the quake, he finally cornered his quarry and was about to jump her, when George Kennedy (a cop, of course) appeared, threw the attacker to the ground, and shot him dead. Consoling the shaking woman, Kennedy said: "I don't know what it is. Earthquakes bring out the worst in some guys."

The other line was much more unusual and exotic so it presented a much greater challenge. It was spoken by Nigel Bruce as Dr. Watson in one of the Sherlock Holmes movies of the 1940s when Watson was attempting to impress a couple on a ship who evidently were not familiar with Holmes's exploits. "Haven't you heard of the giant rat of Sumatra?" asked Watson, referring to one of the great detective's most famous cases. "Haven't you heard of the giant rat of Sumatra?"

Years, decades, passed, and I never came close to a moment when I might work in that line. The degree of difficulty was steep; there were so many elements to the Watson remark. If one heard an opening for the rat, there would still be the matter of its size. If the rat and the size were there, one still had to contend with Sumatra. Above these concerns stood the context. In order to make the question really fit a situation, the opening had to allow for an attitude of superior surprise. "Haven't you heard of the giant rat of Sumatra?" Meaning: "Who has not?"

In the late 1970s I was writing for the *Washington Post*, and I had all but given up on my quest. In all those intervening years not a single conversation had come remotely close to offering me my longed-for opportunity. Then, one day, some friends and I went out to lunch, and it happened to be the fiftieth anniversary of the creation of Mickey Mouse. There was some chatter about Mickey, to which I had been paying scant attention—how much he had contributed to American culture. The usual harmless claptrap. Suddenly, one of the guys sat up with a quizzical look and asked, "Has there ever been a bigger rodent?"

First, I smiled.

In the Madhouse in Beirut

—◊—

When the twelve bombs hit the drab, gray hospital, six people were killed and twenty wounded. Two female patients were sliced to pieces by the shrapnel. The year is 1982, spring. The Beirut hospital is for people suffering from mental and psychological diseases. Among its patients are Lebanese, Palestinians, Maronites, Druze, Sunnis, Shi'ites, and Jews. An Armenian lies curled up on the second floor landing near a lateral gap that looks like an expressionless mouth. Flies collect on his bare feet. Nearby, a young woman cannot control her body. Her arms flail, her legs buckle; she smiles sweetly with her writhing lips. An old woman sits up in bed tearing a round slice of bread to small bits and tossing them on the floor. The children are penned in a small, dark space; they smell of urine; their thighs are stained with excrement. One boy shivers, another laughs. A legless girl spoons mush into the mouth of a younger one. A woman lurches forward and shouts in English: "I am normal!"

I think of these people frequently, even now, twenty years later, as I walk the clean, free beach near my home. I think of them because I cannot help it, and I realize: Be grateful for those you meet who seem the most distant from you, the strangest and most alien. They are the closest.

Should Your Name Appear

—m—

Should your name appear on a list of those about to be executed; should your name appear on a list posted in the town square of citizens slated for execution; should your name be, say, fourth or fifth on the list—there it is, no question of misidentification, it's you, it's your name, sure as shootin'—consider your next step very carefully.

You can, of course, try to escape by boarding the next Greyhound out of town, and, if they haven't blocked the bus stations, train stations, and airports, you'll be in Grand Rapids by nightfall.

You can go to the authorities and protest. You haven't done anything to make them want to execute you. You're innocent, and you can prove it. There must be some mistake.

Mistake! That's it. Another person—one who truly deserves to be executed—happens to share your name. And, indeed, it must be that person, that dop-pelganger, whom the authorities want dead. So, if they would simply go out and find that other person, the one who has your name, well, this mess would be cleared up, and you'd be free as a bird.

Then again, you can always walk up and tear down the list, tear it down and tear it up. And you can take the torn-up list and walk straight up to the authorities and wake them up and tell them that as long as they're up, they can shove it up their asses.

Or you can be executed.

Things I Can Take, Things I Can't

—m—

I can take a punch. Maybe not two punches or three. But one, to the belly or the face. I can take a punch.

And a snub. I've been snubbed a lot, so I know that I can take a snub. Walk past me here. Don't invite me there. I can take it.

I can take extreme heat and extreme cold. The heat was overwhelming in Thailand and in parts of Lebanon and Israel. I climbed the Rock of Masada in a hundred degrees, which was no fun. But I could take it. And the cold, too, in Vermont and New Hampshire, those winters when the gas froze in the tank.

And a slur. I can take a slur. Call me kike, Hebe. I can take that, too, though I'd probably want to find out if *you* can take a punch.

The company of gossips. I can take that, as well. I don't like it, but I can live with it. And the company of fakes and tyrants and amiable accommodators—for brief periods.

Disorder. It's difficult for a Virgo. But I can do it. And nameless fears. I deal with them as well as I can. And shocks, I can take shocks. And I can take a joke.

And ingratitude; I kind of expect it. And cheapness and pettiness. Even rejection. I can take that. And an unlucky streak. Treachery, if you must. It gets me down, but I can take it.

Things I can't take: Your pain, the children's pain, the verdict of your glance.

Relax

—〜—

Everything you did that was worthwhile or worthless will be swallowed up by the same oblivion.

Cliff's Other Notes (More)

De Bello Gallico

Every first-year Latin student learns from Julius Caesar that "all Gaul is divided into three parts." Well, well! All right!

King Lear

It's stupendous, of course. But didn't Lear notice some difference between the characters of his daughters *before* he divvied up the kingdom?

The Prophet

Sophisticates like to make fun of Kahlil Gibran's *The Prophet*. I don't know why. Here, for example, is a typical passage: "Almustafa, the chosen and the beloved, who was a dawn onto his own day, had waited twelve years in the city of Orphalese for his ship that was to return and bear him back to the isle of his birth. And in the twelfth year, on the seventh day of Ielool, the month of reaping, he climbed the hill without the city walls and looked seaward." What's wrong with that, I'd like to know?

The Bible

From John 3:8: "The wind bloweth where it listeth." Excuse me?

Pope

Alexander Pope, the proudest, not to say touchiest of men, wrote: "Thus let me love, unseen, unknown; thus unlamented let me die; steal from the world, and not a stone tell where I lie." The stone would have been unnecessary. Here's where he lied.

Shakespeare

If you wish to impress your friends, you can interrupt them every time they unknowingly quote Shakespeare. Here's a sampler: "The dogs of war"; "a charmed life"; "yeoman's service"; "thereby hangs the tale"; "foul play"; "melted...into thin air"; "cold comfort"; "my mind's eye"; "for ever and a day"; "one fell swoop"; and "lay on, Macduff"—for which one has to know someone named Macduff.

Tocqueville and Dr. Johnson

Even though it is de rigueur to quote either or both of these men in any speech or article, they were not the same person. Johnson, particularly, has been misrepresented in history, mainly because Boswell was easily amused, and so he played up the wise guy in Johnson—"Sir," this and "Sir," that—followed by what passed for a zinger in eighteenth-century London. The real Dr. Johnson was a physically unattractive, tormented man who had a psychotic fear of death and yet showed a magnificent affinity for the underclass, of which he was one. If you want to quote the real Johnson, try this: "The test of a civilization is how it treats its poor."

Kafka's *The Metamorphosis*

Probably about a hangover, but still mesmerizing.

Jane Eyre, Wuthering Heights, and *Rebecca*

As much fun as these three novels are individually, think how exciting they would be if they were combined. Heathcliff storms after Rebecca, who laughs in his face; he kills her. Maxim de Winter marries Jane Eyre and treats her miserably. Rochester hires

Catherine Earnshaw, who becomes his first wife and sets fire to the house, aided by Mrs. Danvers, who has set fire to Heathcliff's house. Everybody has a great time, and there is lots of sturming and dranging. And all packed into a single book that in no way violates the original three, which no one can figure out anyway. Narrated by Ethan Frome. Just a suggestion.

The Inventor of Time

If no one had invented time, everything would happen all at once. Your birth, your schooling, your preposterous behavior at the prom, your marriage, the birth of your children, the scorn of your children, your éclaircissements, your denouements—all would occur in the blink of an eye, and everything in life would be accordioned like the paper sheath of a drinking straw, just before a drop of water turns it into a writhing snake.

But this simile is so inadequate. It is impossible to imagine a world without time, where no time hangs heavy, and no hands have time on them, and no one serves time because time serves no one, and there are neither the best of times nor the worst.

Someone, you see, had to think it up—a Cro-Magnon, perhaps, after he had knocked off the Neanderthals because they could not speak and were a waste of something—perhaps one who noticed that this moment was not like the previous moment and who conjectured that the next moment, the moment to come, was likely to be different as well.

I like to think of that person: The mother-to-be who watched her belly swell from month to month and realized that something miraculous was going to emerge; the artist who, displeased with the red ox he had just painted on the wall of his cave, realized that he could do another picture later; or the hunter who, as the lion was about to leap on his head, realized that something was not on his side.

I could spend hours wondering who that person was, and how he or she realized in a flash of invention, that from then on, there would be a then on, and a there was, and an is.

Oh, hell. I'll say what I mean. I want more time.

Explanation to an Unprincipled Employer

—◦—

The monumental degree of athletic difficulty you will encounter when attempting it; the excruciating lower-back pain, nerve pain, and muscle pain you will have as body parts are made to do what they were never meant to do; the exposing nakedness required of you and the shattering embarrassment and humiliation you will suffer should passers-by catch you in the act; the unique conclusion, ending in no pleasure whatsoever, but rather in the opposite, a heaving sorrow, full of gasping and despair, especially when you realize that word of this will get abroad and that others will remind you of your ignoble behavior for all eternity. *That* is why I told you to go fuck yourself.

Signs of Accomplishment as Depicted in the Rear Window of a Volvo

—⁄⁄—

Groton; Harvard; Ambition; Infatuation; Love; Marriage; Ambition; Self-Inspection; Weakness; Doubt; Disintegration; Fear; Children; Ambition; Groton; Harvard.

A Valediction for All Occasions

Good-bye.

A Brief History of Idiocy

—✺—

Let's throw a party.

The Intervention of Facts

—◠—

She says: The first known bird is the archaeopteryx.

He says: The Chinese invented the clock.

She says: Larry Doby was the second Negro League player to make it to the majors.

He says: Gyula is a town on the White Koros River near the Romanian border.

She says: I paid the AmEx bill on time.

He says: They say you didn't, and there's going to be a late charge.

She says: They are in error.

He says: There will be penalties.

She says: Fine.

He says: Fine, and flushed with anger, he goes to the bookshelf to take down the *The Official Encyclopedia of Baseball*.

You Think I'm Kidding

Here's what I don't like. I don't like knowing that I will have lived sixty, seventy, or eighty years without having rid the world of barbarians, tyrants, traitors, bullies, murderers, liars, thieves, crooks, and backbiters. What's more, I will not have cured all the world's diseases, from the sniffles to the Ebola virus. Neither will I have prevented droughts, floods, and earthquakes. I will not have eradicated world poverty and famine. I will not have put an end to injustice, or even to casual cruelty.

I will not have established freedom and goodwill everywhere. I will not have seen to it that everyone leads a useful and productive life and exhibits only tenderness and generosity toward others—all others. I will not have unified the races, or equalized the genders, or protected and educated the children. Nothing I will have done will have resulted in a complete world reformation. In all my sixty, seventy, or eighty years—nothing. And that's what I don't like.

You think I'm kidding.

Ashley Montana Goes Ashore in the Caicos

—*m*—

The cover of a Sports Illustrated *swimsuit issue shows a gorgeous blond, Ashley Montana, emerging from the sea, wearing a white bathing suit and a white straw hat. She appears to be bone dry. The caption reads:* ASHLEY MONTANA GOES ASHORE IN THE CAICOS.

We are aboard my sailing yacht, Ashley Montana and I. I, too, am named Ashley Montana, as is the boat. We are all three called Ashley Montana. Ashley and I have just made love four times in the past fifteen minutes. She is pooped. I am full of pep and vim. She stretches out on the poop deck and veils her vague blue eyes behind the lenses of her oversize Porsche sunglasses.

"Pooped?" I ask.

"Bored," she barely says.

The word terrifies me. If Ashley is bored, she is bored with *me*. I know it's true.

It was not so in the beginning, when love was young. Or as she put it, when the "relationship" was young. In those days, Ashley and I were *new*, everything was *new*. We were modern life itself! How the time flew by! We would lunch alfresco at those cramped, tiny restaurants on Madison Avenue with the little tables spilling out onto the middle of the sidewalk. We stared past each other and ordered water. How gaunt we looked! How pained!

We read celebrity magazines from cover to cover. Often it took days. Yet we knew everything one could possibly know about Ben Affleck and J. Lo and Rosie and Chris Matthews. Our heads swam with knowledge.

We took up ceramics. We bought each other stuffed animals. We gave them names! We called them both Ashley. We were invited to benefits for serious diseases. We went! How we laughed!

We threw each other surprise birthday parties, where everyone brought hilarious gifts and everyone made hilarious toasts, and weren't we both surprised! Guests came dressed as their favorite diet. Such fun guessing.

We watched *Law and Order.* We watched *Law and Order.* We watched *Law and Order.*

We watched *Masterpiece Theater.* We saw another thirty-part series on the collapse of the British Empire. Britain had to give India back to India. We wept for weeks.

We were on TV ourselves. We did the news. "Back to you." She said, "Back to you." I said, "No, back to *you.*" We were journalists.

We did a lot of soul-searching. No luck so far.

We talked about our latest projects with other people. We talked about *their* projects. So many screenplays, so many movies of the week, docudramas, miniseries, so many first novels. (We had always wanted to write one.) We redid the kitchen. (We could not use the apartment for a year!) We bought land in Montana. That made Ashley happy. We re-nounced Ecstasy though neither of us had ever taken any. We were ecstatic. Nonetheless, we admitted our-selves to the Betty Ford Clinic. Everyone said it was a beautiful gesture. It made the columns.

We *found* ourselves. We *lost* ourselves. We *found* ourselves again. We *lost* ourselves again. Someone found ourselves *for* us and returned them, but demanded a reward. We learned how to *be* ourselves. We learned how to be *other* people. Other people learned how to be *us*. It was confusing.

We had breakthroughs and breakdowns and breakfast. We cleaned up our act. We were in a time warp. We were in a wormhole. We were in a worm warp. We were burned out. We reached critical mass. We experienced rapprochements and schadenfreude and vertigo and *Fahrvergnügen*. And déjàs vu. We had the flu. We decided to go somewhere completely different for the summer, at first, but in the end, well, when would we see our friends? We air-kissed everybody and everybody air-kissed us.

We were OK. I was OK, and she was OK. We asked each other. "You OK?" We were.

We came on to each other. We had it all together. We got on with our lives. We told each other: "Go for it!" *It!* We were there for each other. *There!* Our energy was palpable, our atmosphere electric. We refused to learn from history, and thus we were bound to repeat it.

We were state of the art. We were on the cutting edge. We had our priorities straight. We had our heads on straight. We empowered each other. We crossed the line. We parented. We weren't parents, but we parented anyway—because we were superpersons: We were bank presidents in the morning, coached Little League in the afternoon, cooked coq au vin in the evening and were on-line all night. I don't know *how* we did it.

We were caring persons. We cared for *us*.

We *saw* Penn & Teller. We *shopped* at Dean & DeLuca. We *called* Jacoby & Meyers. We *knew* Crabtree & Evelyn. Well, we knew Evelyn. We knew Sy Syms. We were educated consumers. We were his best customers.

We had wellness. We had Botox. We had liposuction. We had hipposuction. We had rhinoplasty. We had elephantiasis.

We lost thirty pounds with Ultra Slim-Fast. We got gravely ill.

We woke up and smelled the coffee. It was Starbucks, from Rio, Rio Grande. We asked each other, "Whazzup?" "Zup?" "What up?" It was *us*. *We* were up.

We were laid back. We were uptight. We were ripped off. We were on a roll. We were in a rut. We were boss! We were fly! We were bitchin'! We were dudes! Didn't you just love us? We got *every* joke that David Letterman made. We knew the names of *every* rock band on *Saturday Night Live*. We liked the way they *dressed*.

We had brunch!

We ate shiitake mushrooms and buffalo wings and a terrine of carpaccio with a paillard of chicken.

We fought for animal rights. We opposed capital punishment. We opposed capital punishment for animals. A pussycat was electrocuted in Texas. A serial killer. Mice, mostly. We held a vigil.

We collected Judy Chicago. We collected Robert Indiana. We loved Tennessee Williams. We admired George Washington. Naturally, we were crazy about Ashley Montana. And Joe Montana. And Joe Montegna.

We were *above* the law. We were *below* the fold. We were *beyond* the pale. We were *under* a great deal of pressure. We were *around* the block. We were *over* the hill. We were *beside* ourselves. We were *beneath* contempt.

We were into yoga. We were into yogurt. We were into prepositions.

We were plugged in. We were tuned out. We networked. We faced. We interfaced. We uploaded. We downloaded. We got loaded. We were caught in the World Wide Web.

We were Eurocentric. We were Eurotrash. We faded in. We faded out. We cut to the chase. They picked up our option.

We did construction work. We did *de*construction work. We bought weapons of mass deconstruction. We were radiant, luminous. Both radiant *and* luminous.

Our phone-answering machine left exceptionally clever messages. The phone never stopped ringing. The phone rang off the hook. We received calls from cars, from planes, from briefcases.

We had eyeglasses made in one hour.

We lost our contacts.

We lost contact. We began to bicker. We began to find each other disappointing. We began to judge each other inappropriate.

I wanted to switch to Verizon; she wanted to stay with AT&T. I said Certs was a candy mint. *She* said it was a breath mint. I said her shoes looked like a pump. *She* said they felt like a sneaker. I said: "Tastes great." *She* said, "Less filling."

We fought over the career of Ed McMahon. We argued whether Ed had been a slave to Johnny or a star in his own right.

Could we both be right? We made up. We vowed to have no more big dinner parties. We did the right thing. We had a nice day. We had a good one.

And then, suddenly, it was all gone. Gone. And now...

Lately, I have tried without success to attract Ashley's interest. She says everything is boring. I attempt to engage her in politics. Boring, she says. I show her a photograph of Attorney General John Ashcroft. I read her the latest biography of a dead U.S. President. I turn on the PBS series on the American ice cream cone. Ten parts. Lots of postcards. Boring, she says.

The world of current events, which enchants me completely, sets her to yawning. Nuances of language, which have me mesmerized, hold her not. Books, movies, the antics of public figures, all of which make me leap for joy, are nothing to Ashley. I try to bring back the old days. I sing her "Macho Man." She looks away. I sing "Kumbaya." She says she's never heard of it.

Now, on our boat, the *Ashley Montana*, I plead with her. "Don't be bored, darling," I say. "Let's find an island. A place for us. Somewhere." We had already visited ten such islands. One was on the Perillo Tours. Yet none of the islands had truly seized Ashley's fancy—an illusive thing, to be sure. Nonetheless, the idea perks her up.

"Aruba?" I suggest. She shakes her head no. "Anguilla?" I offer. She rolls her eyes skyward. "St. Barths? St. Kitts? St. Croix?" Not a nod.

Ashley says, "How about Portosan?"

I explain to her that Portosan is not an island.

"How about the Caicos?" she says.

"Never heard of them," I retort.

She sits bolt upright. "Never *heard* of them? Never heard of the *Caicos*?" She explodes in laughter so shrill it scatters the fish.

"Ashley, Ashley," she sighs woefully. "*Everybody* knows the Caicos. The Caicos are *it!* Tom Cruise goes there. Penelope Cruz is there right *now.* On a cruise. Claus von Bülow, Lizzie Grubman, Norman Mailer. *All* the best people. Look, I'm sorry. But if you've never heard of the Caicos, what's the point, I'd like to know, of us going on?"

It is the moment I have dreaded. Shamelessly I beg her to stay with me. But I can see that she's ready to jump ship. It was plain from the start: She has her world, I mine.

"Go," I tell her. "But stay dry."

"Good-bye, Ashley," she says, and jumps overboard.

For a minute or so I watch her swim toward shore, in her hat, the water beading—and immediately evaporating—on her swimsuit as she glides through the sea. Soon she is far away. I turn my yacht about and sail north. I am heartbroken, yet enlightened, and full of warm memories of our time together—while in the distance, with the sun full upon the sea, and the air as free as a dream, Ashley Montana goes ashore in the Caicos.

How to Live in the World

—⁓—

These instructions come in French and Japanese as well, and in other languages, but don't let that throw you. Don't let anything about the enterprise throw you. You can do it, anyone can do it, because one really doesn't live in the world when it comes down to it (and it always comes down to it). Rather, one waits for the world to live in you—as a composer waits for rapture, and then becomes the life he seeks.

But, if that sounds a bit abstract to you, a little hoity-toity, read that part of *Specimen Days* in which nurse Walt Whitman is attending the Union fallen and near-dead in the U.S. Patent Office in Washington, D.C., which doubled as a hospital during the Civil War—where he notes, with barely a critical remark, that the same species capable of coming up with the most dazzling inventions made of wood and brass was just as capable of blowing off one another's limbs. The hall was filled with bright machines side by side with men on cots, massaging their new stumps.

It is the way you feel when listening to national politicians speak of our great power and our powerful greatness while in your heart, you recall that still and airless afternoon in Africa, when you held an eleven-year-old in your arms shortly after he had died of starvation. Light as a feather. His last breath went out of him like a drop from a vial.

So, how to live in the world? Wait till the end of the day, when the family of swans has sequestered itself under the drawbridge near the NO WAKE sign, and the light has stalled above the open mouth of the creek, so that the sun burns like a coal in ash, and the wind is a rumor on your face, your limbs, and you are filled with wonder and remorse. Then go treat the wounded.

Aubade

—⁓—

Inseparable from the dark dawn, this white chair, stained
brown-orange at the top of the back cushion, and the
ink scratches on its arms. This yellow pad. This Bic
  without its top.
This silence and these words that remain silent yet push and
  elbow
each other out of the way like Hollywood extras vying for
  attention. These dreams
that go forward and back, past scoundrels and geese in great
flights and the outrages of history, which, since they are
  dreams,
become birds, then baseballs, then blues numbers and my
  dad in his kitchen, singing show tunes in his slippers.
This morning, this life. One could die of happiness.

Instructions to the Pallbearers

—◁∿▷—

Use the casket for a planter. I never did like boxes. Instead, prop me up on a high place where I can face the water—a bay, not an ocean—so that boats may pass before my blind eyes, and the noise of children playing on a float may attack my deaf ears. Then leave me to rot. And, keep the worms away, if you can. Death ought to be different.

On the Other Hand

—m—

On the other hand, rejoice. The heat from the fire has blistered the blue paint on your door, and the ashes from the volcano are floating like chicken feathers everywhere, and the mouth of the earthquake has swallowed up the silver and the books, and as soon as the tsunami arrives, there will be nothing left—no piano, no red vase from Italy, no antique Shaker shovel, no tennis trophy—not even a photo ID to tell you who you are.

But this, I will remind you, is what you wanted—to be free of possessions, to reflect on the worthiness of life, to be as noble as the heart allows. And, ID or no, you know who you are.

The Grateful Living

At last: A clean, clear image. The sunlight on a gull; the gull on a piling; the piling on a channel. The channel noses through to the open bay, and the bay to the sea. But I don't need to go there now. The gull is enough, plenty. I don't see why eternity has to go on forever. Here is my place in the world.

Thank you. Thank you and you and you.

ACKNOWLEDGMENTS

I have two editors-in-chief. One, Ginny Rosenblatt, first saw my work forty years ago and felt that it needed so much editing, she married me. The other, Jane Isay, who doubles as editor-in-chief of Harcourt, while not going as far as Ginny, has joined the effort toward my improvement with great skill and gusto. I thank them heartily and wish them continued good luck.

Thanks as well to Gloria Loomis, my agent of twenty-seven years, who keeps at it in spite of her better judgment and to Jane Freeman, my artist-transcriber, who translates my work from the original Sanskrit and who also makes so many helpful suggestions, I begin to resent them.

An old high-school teacher of mine is cited in one of these essays. Jon Beck Shank was a poet, a great, good heart, and a gift to those lucky enough to learn from him. I'm forever grateful for his words of encouragement spoken so many long, winding years ago.

Roger Rosenblatt